René Novella

THE PRINCIPALITY OF MONACO

Preface by

H.R.H. PRINCE RAINIER III

Preface by
H.R.H. PRINCE RAINIER III

A great deal has been written about the principality; therefore the appearance of a new book shortly after the publication of the «History of Monaco» is not surprising.

The Bonechi Publishing House did a remarkable job: the quality of the presentation is accompanied by an accurate text, illustrated by magnificent photographs, and one is absorbed from the beginning to end.

Unlike heavy history books or commonplace tourist guide-books, this books revives the past, transmitting to all readers, after a tour of the Principality, the same pleasure as a passing guest.

Monaco: maybe a Dream, but also a Reality and a Principality that progresses... Deo Juvante as the author justly recalls.

I wish this book all the success it deserves and congratulate its authors.

May 1989

René Novella, temporary Italian ambassador and plenipotentiary to His Serene Highness the Prince of Monaco, was born in Monaco on February 6, 1922.

On his mother's side he descended from an old Monégasque family whose ancestors came to the principality at the time of Prince Honoré II and constructed, among other things, the chapel of the Prince's Palace and the Chapel of Mercy of the Archiconfraternity of Penitents.

After his elementary and secondary schooling at the Lycée of Monaco, Novella attended the University of Aix-Marseilles where he studied humanities. After his formal studies he devoted himself to teaching.

His acquaintance with Curzio Malaparte, of whom he became the principal translator (The Skin, L'Uovo Rosso, Donna come me, Sangue, Sodoma e Gomorra), was to bring him into contact with the publishing world. He also translated the works of Matteo Bandello and Antonio Aniante.

He was successively employed as general secretary of the Editions du Rocher, director of editions at the Polygraphic Institute of Monaco, and director of the Library of Monaco; he was subsequently nominated cultural and conferential attaché, and later attaché of public education, youth and sport.

In addition to his present career, Novella presides over the National Monegasque Commission for UNESCO, the International Accademy of Dialects, and the Committee for the Monegasque Language.

A member of the International Committee for the French Language, he is active on various administrative councils and cultural organizations, and for over 30 years has taken part in organizing the International Television Festival of Monte Carlo.

He is the author of numerous prefaces and articles on the history of literature in collective works, and has written various books on the Principality of Monaco.

The photographs were taken specially for this volume by GIANNI DAGLI ORTI.

Palais de Monaco

On a beaucoup écrit sur la Principauté, aussi la parution d'un nouvel ouvrage au moment où venait d'être éditée la récente "Histoire de Monaco" pouvait-elle surprendre.

La réalisation des Editions Bonechi est remarquable, elle allie à la qualité de la présentation un texte soigné et précis, illustré de magnifiques photographies, dont l'ensemble retient l'intérêt de bout en bout.

S'il est de très austères livres d'histoire, s'il est de très banals guides touristiques, ce livre, au contraire, rend vivantes les évocations historiques du passé et communique à chacun, après sa promenade à travers la Principauté, le même plaisir qu'à un hôte de passage.

Monaco un Rêve, sans doute, mais aussi une Réalité, une Principauté qui avance ... Deo Juvante comme le rappelle si justement l'auteur.

Je souhaite à cette réalisation le succès qu'elle mérite et exprime à ses auteurs mes sincères félicitations.

Mai 1989.

To H.R.H. Prince Rainier III,
on the 40th anniversary of
his ascent to the Grimaldi throne.

View from the Rock of the Exotic Garden.

HISTORY

PREHISTORY – THE LIGURIANS – ANCIENT TIMES – INVASIONS

The fact that Monaco has been inhabited since the late Paleolithic Age, approximately 3000 BC, has been proven by finds brought to light in Monaco itself and in neighbouring villages.

Ligurians from eastern Europe invaded the coastal area from Tuscany to the Rhone in about 2000 BC. They introduced their language, an Indo-European derivative, and developed trade with the Phoenicians, Carthaginians and, later on, the Greeks.

The name of Monaco was first mentioned by Periegesis of Hecate in Miletus who, when listing the major built up areas in the northern Mediterranean basin from west to east, mentioned Narbonne, Marseilles, Monoikos Polis Ligustike *(Monaco, town in Liguria), Intemelium and the island of Elba.*

During the 2nd century BC, the Romans conquered Liguria and what was Monaco at the time was called Portus Herculis Monoeci.

The importance of this natural bay where sailors moored their ships is accentuated in texts by Virgil, Strabo, Lucan and Tacitus.

At the time of the martyrdom of heretics, the body of a young Corsican victim, Dévote was found at the outlet of the Gaumates valley, on the site of the church which the Monacans then dedicated to their patron saint.

After the decline of Rome, the Lombards devastated the Ligurian coast. During the 6th, 7th and 8th Centuries, Mohammedan pirates touched on the coast during their raids.

It was not until the 10th Century that this hazard disappeared and it was only then that the peoples who had fled inland returned to settle on the Mediterranean coasts.

THE GENOESE

As from the 11th Century, the Republic of Genoa extended its authority right throughout Liguria and the emperor Frederick Barbarossa granted the Genoese mastery of the seas from Portovenere to Monaco.

As from 1215, the Genoese were assigned the port and Rock; in accordance with the gold imperial seal, they started building on the site of the current palace a castle encompassed by four towers interconnected by a bastion.

In 1252 the Church of St. Nicholas was built on the Rock in Romanesque style.

At the beginning of the 13th Century Monaco was afflicted by the wars in Genoa between the Guelphs, who backed the Pope, and the Ghibellines, in support of the Emperor.

Largillière:
Portrait of Jack I Prince of Monaco.

H. Rigaud:
Portrait of Anthony I Prince of Monaco.

THE GRIMALDIS

It was in the wake of a battle lost by the Guelphs that Francis Grimaldi, known as Malizia, on his way back to Provence, tricked his way into Monaco castle on the night of the 8th January 1297 with his men dressed up as Franciscan monks, taking possession of it.

He was driven away some years later but, since then, the two bare-footed, bearded, long-haired monks with their swords drawn feature in the Grimaldi coat-of arms, together with the tapered silver and red shield.

The descendants of Otto Canella, the Genoese consul who died in 1143, had taken on as a patronymic the name of Grimaldo, elected Genoese consul three times and son of Otto Canella.

Rainier I, great-grandson of Otto Canella and French admiral who defeated the Flemish in the Battle of Zierikzee, is considered the founder of the Grimaldi of Monaco dynasty, despite the fact that he never managed to enter Monaco, renconquered in 1331 by his son Charles who also took possession of the seigniories of Menton and Roquebrune.

Charles I, warrior and sailor at the service of the King of France, took part in the Battle of Crécy and the Siege of Calais. He died during the Siege of Monaco led by the doge of Genoa, Simon Boccanegra. Monaco fell into the hands of the Genoese as did Roquebrune; howerer, the Grimaldis kept Menton, where they remained while waiting to seize Monaco.

In 1407 Rainier II regained possession of Roquebrune.

His three sons – Ambrose, Anthony and John – took advantage of a Ghibelline defeat to reinstate the Seigniory of Monaco in 1419 and each ruled in turn for a year until John I became the only Lord of Monaco. He guaranteed its independence by offering his services to his neighbours: Provence, Savoy, Genoa, Milan and France, depending on how powerful they were at the time. This policy of maintaining the balance of power, continued by his successors, ensured Monaco's survival until the French Revolution.

Emprisoned by the Duke of Milan who threatened to kill him if he did not hand over his Seigniory, John I asked his wife Pomelline to resist. She courageously obeyed her husband, who was then finally freed.
Upon the death of John I, his son Catalan became sovereign of Monaco. But he only reigned for three years and before dying, he appointed his mother Pomelline as his successor; she was then succeeded by her

Attributed to Louis Tocquet:
Portrait of Honoré III Prince of Monaco.

F. Biard:
Portrait of Charles III Prince of Monaco.

younger daughter Claudine, destined to marry her cousin Lambert Grimaldi, sovereign of Menton.

A fierce struggle ensued between Pomelline and Lambert, who married Claudine when she turned fifteen; she bore fourteen children.

Lambert, an astute diplomat and cunning strategist, strengthened Monaco's position by sticking to the balance of power policy but also by extending his alliances beyond his neighbours.

His son John II followed in his footsteps and strengthened the good relations established by Lambert with Charles VIII, King of France.

After a quarrel, he was killed by his son Lucian. The latter's good faith was never put to the question.

Lucian displayed his courage by resisting for one hundred days and thwarting a siege of Monaco on the part of the Genoese.

Louis XII sent him letters acknowledging that «the Seigniory of Monaco is held only by God and the sword». He in turn was assassinated with the complicity of Andrea Doria.

Augustine Grimaldi, Bishop of Grasse, succeeded his brother for life. He tried to strengthen the alliance with France but action on the part of Francis I forced him to negotiate the treaties of Burgos and Tordesillas with Charles V in 1524, following on which Monaco became a Spanish protectorate.

Upon the death of Augustine in 1532, Lucian's son Honoré I was still under age. His guardian was Stephen Grimaldi, known as the Governor, who further strengthened the alliance with Spain, doing his utmost to make Monaco as independent as possible.

In this way, Stephen ruled supreme until he died, with the approval of Honoré who was to continue the same policy during the twenty years in which he actually reigned.

Hard times marked by intrigues and conflicts were to follow for the son of Honoré I, Charles II, and his son Hercules I.

Upon Hercules I's violent death, once again a minor came to the throne of Monaco: Honoré II. Prince Frederick of Valdetare, his tutor, convinced him to take on the title of prince.

The young sovereign, educated with a taste for literature, art and the cult of grandeur, renovated the palace, which he filled with art and valuable collections. He had coins minted in his own image and commenced a reconciliation with France through

L. Bonnat:
Portrait of Albert I Prince of Monaco.

P. Laszlo:
Portrait of Louis II Prince of Monaco.

Richelieu.

In 1641 he signed the Treaty of Péronne with Louis XIII, guaranteeing the friendship and protection of France. The Spaniards were expelled from Monaco. Honoré was received at the court of France with art and valuable collections. He had coins minted in his own image and commenced a reconciliation with France through Richelieu.

In 1641 he signed the Treaty of Péronne with Louis XIII, guaranteeing the friendship and protection of France. The Spaniards were expelled from Monaco. Honoré was received at the court of France with great pomp and ceremony and King Louis XIV became godfather to his grandson, the future Louis I.

At the Monaco palace, sumptuous balls continued right throughout his reign.

In 1662 he was suceeded by Louis I, after his brilliant debut at the French court where he met his future wife, Charlotte, dauther of Marshal De Gramont. He offered his services to the king of France, took part in the United Provinces war against England and, at the head of his Monaco-Cavalry regiment, he participated in the campaign of Flanders and Franche-Comté.

In his desire to guarantee the succession of the Spanish king Charles II to his daughter Maria Theresa, King Louis XIV chose him as ambassador at the Holy See on account of his diplomacy and numerous cardinal relatives.

Louis I spent part of his wealth to make his embassy as sumptuous as possible. He died in Rome in 1701.

His son Anthony I came to the Grimaldi throne at the age of forty. In the past, he had distinguished himself on the battlefield at Fleurus, Mons and Namur, where his courage and stature won him the nick-name of Goliath.

An accomplished musician, he directed his orchestra with the stick left to him by Lully and organised a sizeable library of musical works. In fear of an invasion, he fortified the Palace and the point of the Rock peninsula.

His daughter, Louise-Hippolyte, married Jacques-François-Léonor of Goyon-Matignon. She only reigned for a couple of months before dying of smallpox.

17th Century French school: Portrait of Hercules Grimaldi, Prince of Monaco and Marquis de Champagne, at the age of thirteen.

James I soon abdicated in favour of his son Honoré III, who was still under age; he remained his guardian having appointed as governor of the principality Chevalier de Grimaldi, the natural son of Anthony I.

At the beginning of his reign, Honoré III participated in the campaign of Flanders, the Rhine and the Netherlands. He spent most of his time in Paris and in Normandy, entrusting dutiful Chevalier de Grimaldi with the government of Monaco.

The principality then went through a long period of peace, interrupted only by the block imposed from October 1746 to June 1747 by the empress Maria Theresa and by the King of Sardinia Charles Emmanuel III, who were not convinced by Honoré III's declaration of neutrality.

Mastery of the sea, sea traffic and fishing contributed to the local economy. Citrus fruit was grown. The first industries and a printing works came into being. Art and literature were given a substantial boost.

However, new ideas from France angered the townsfolk of Menton and Roquebrune. Prince Honoré III wreaked his revenge to a certain extent but the fall of the French monarchy and the severing of diplomatic ties between France and Sardinia brought the French troops to Monaco, where they set up a people's society which declared the fall of the Grimaldis. With the proclamation of the republic, annexation to France was requested.

On 4th February 1793, the Convention voted the union of the principality with France. The palace was looted and turned into a military barracks, and then a poorhouse.

Prince Honoré was incarcerated, along with all the members of his family. His daughter-in-law, Françoise de Choiseul-Stainville was guillotined at the age of twenty-seven.

Freed in October 1794, Honoré III died a couple of months later.

During the Napoleonic age, his grandchildren served in the French army.

After Napoleon abdicated, Prince Honoré IV, son of Honoré III, staked his claim. Once ill, he delegated his powers to his brother Joseph and then to his elder son who reigned under the name of Honoré V.

After the Hundred Days, the Congress of Vienna placed the principality under the protectorate of the King of Sardinia.

Honoré V tried courageously to face the financial difficulties of the restoration by creating industrial and artisan activities and by granting certain monopolies, in particular wheat and flour monopolies. This system, considered «exclusive», led to the dissension of the people due to the secession of the Communes of Menton and Roquebrune.

On his death bed, Honoré V composed his own epitaph, which sums up perfectly the action of a difficult, yet generous, reign: «Here lies he who meant well».

He was succeeded by his brother Florestan I, a man of letters and a liberal. He abolished the monopoly policy, but in Menton and Roquebrune the situation was coming to a head and in 1848 the two Communes declared themselves free towns.

Despite his popularity, the crown prince Charles, who visited the towns of unrest where he could count on the aid of countless admirers, never managed to prevent the two towns from being attached to France, right at the time when it was annexing the county of Nice and Savoy.

On the death of Prince Florestan on 26th June 1856, Prince Charles III, who had been administering the principality for some years with the help of his mother Princess Caroline, signed with Napoleon III the treaty of the 2nd February 1861. Its main clauses ensured the independence of the principality, ratified once and for all the loss of Menton and Roquebrune, stipulated the payment of a compensatory indemnity and established the construction of a coast road between Nice and Monaco and the passing of the Nice-Genoa railway over the territory of the principality. In 1865 a French-Monacan agreement settled the procedures of the customs union and relations between the two countries.

Even before the death of Prince Florestan, Prince Charles II and Princess Caroline had made several attempts to industrialize the principality in order to bottom out of the recession. They had all gone up in smoke apart from attempts at exploiting the country's favourable climatic conditions, at the time that the Côte d'Azur was coming into full swing.

In 1866, a new district came into being in front of the Grimaldi rock. It was called Monte Carlo after Prince Charles III and soon became synonymous with parties, elegance, shows, leisure and sports.

Direct taxes were suppressed. The worlds of politics, literature and arts met in the principality. Prince Charles III created the Order of Saint Charles, minted gold coins, issued the first Monacan stamps, opened legations and consulates abroad, signed bilateral treaties with major European countries and obtained from the Holy See the religious independence of the principality, which then became a bishopric.

Justice, the police and teaching underwent considerable reforms.

When Prince Charles III died on 10th September 1889, he left his son Albert a modern state that fitted perfectly well into the new Europe.

The crown prince Albert had dedicated his youth to sailing and science and his coming to power did not thwart these interests. Prince Albert I followed in his father's footsteps, adding a scientific dimension.

During his reign, art flourished with the unforgettable creation of operas and the installation of the Diaghilev Russian ballets in Monaco.

In the political field, Prince Albert I granted the first constitution; he signed a friendly agreement with France settling dynastic problems and redefining the customs union, not to mention countless international agreements with other countries.

He turned the principality into an international meeting place and in 1903 he founded the International Peace Institute for the peaceful settlement of conflicts.

In Paris he set up the Oceanographic Institute and the Institute of Human Paleontology whereas in Monaco he founded the Oceanographic Museum, the Museum of Prehistoric Paleontology and the Exotic Garden.

He modernized the port, had the government buildings erected, opened a grammar school, created a girls' boarding school and schools, had a new hospital built and organised air displays, motor-boat races and the first Monte Carlo car rally.

Corresponding member of the French Scientific Academy and French Academy of Medicine and holder of the Agassiz medal, Prince Albert I died on 26th June 1922.

His son, Prince Louis II, who had distinguished himself in the ranks of the French army during the First World War on account of his heroic acts, directed Monacan politics during the difficult period during the two World Wars and the long economic recession, which ended with the Second World War.

Despite the double occupation of Monte Carlo, he preserved the work of his predecessors by pursuing a policy of independence and cultural, economic and social development. He created the medical-juridical commission for humanitarian purposes and, in the field of information, Radio Monte Carlo broadcasting station. In 1929, during his reign, the first Grand Prix in Monaco came into being.

When he died in 1949, he was succeeded by his grandson, Prince Rainier III, son of Princess Charlotte and Prince Pierre, Count of Polignac. At twenty-six, he started one of the greatest reigns in the history of Monaco.

Having served in the French army, once he came of age Prince Rainier already knew the ropes of the Monacan administration which was developing rapidly under his guidance.

He increased the national territory by one-fifth of its surface by means of spectacular constructions over the sea. He was responsible for creating new scientific institutions: the Scientific Centre, the Acclimatization Zoological Centre and the Larvotto Underwater Reserve hosting the Marine Radioactivity Laboratories. Furthermore, he launched a real crusade against marine pollution, equipped Monte Carlo with a long sandy beach, established a quick network across the whole territory thanks to an underground railway, renewed the road network by tunnelling through the Rock, linked the various districts of the built up area vertically, modernized the Bas-Moulins districts and urbanized Fontvieille where a new stadium, church, public facilities, school facilities, heliport, council housing and industrial premises were built.

He gave the Monacans a new Constitution. Moreover, he signed new agreements with France, various bilateral treaties with other European countries and several multilateral treaties.

During his reign, the principality belonged to major international organisations; all legations in Monaco were raised to the rank of embassy and the bishop was made Archbishop. The cultural Order of Merit was then instituted to reward artistic talents and the Grimaldi Order for services rendered to the Head of State and for contributing to the principality's renown throughout the world.

Economic develpment was favoured by the extension of hotel accommodation and the diversification of tourist activities, extended to business tourism and congresses, thanks to the creation of the International Meetings Centre and the Congress Centre Auditorium of Monaco.

It was likewise stimulated by a powerful industrial and commercial sector basically consisting of high value added activities that require highly trained staff and a risk minimum.

However, services in transport, banks, media and technical design and link departments expanded most rapidly.

Their royal highnesses
Prince Rainier III
and the crown Prince Albert.

Approximately 22.000 employees, of whom one-third reside outside the principality, and about 3.300 State agents form the work force.

To encourage literature, art and science, Prince Rainier III instituted the Prince Peter of Monaco literary price, the Prince Peter of Monaco Music Composition Prize, the Contemporary Art Prize and the Albert I Oceanographic Prize.

In the media field, having ensured the extension of Radio Monte Carlo thanks to the installation of powerful transmitters in the Haute Provence Alps, Prince Rainier III created Tele Monte Carlo station and instituted the International Monte Carlo Television Festival to favour exceptional contributions to information and for the enjoyment of people worldwide.

On her part, Princess Grace of Monaco created the Monte Carlo Flower Show, Garden Club and Festival of Arts, now Spring of the Arts, chaired by Princess Caroline.

Since the dreadful accident that took place on the 13th September 1982 resulting in the death of Princess Grace the following day, the Foundation that bears her name has been chaired by Princess Caroline, whereas presidency of the Red Cross, that she had been responsible for since her marriage, was assigned to crown prince Albert.

Some years after the seventh centenary of the arrival of the Grimaldis in Monaco and at the dawn of the third millenary of our era, Prince Rainier III still pursues the work done by his ancestors, faithful to their motto «DEO JUVANTE».

Overview of the Prince's Palace.

THE PALACE

The history of the Prince's palace more or less corresponds to that of the Grimaldis.

In 1162, the Emperor Frederick I Barbarossa granted the Republic of Genoa mastery of the sea over the Ligurian coast from Monaco to Porto Venere. On 30th May 1191, by means of a golden seal, Emperor Henry VI granted him, in exchange for vassalage to the Empire, the ownership of the port and Rock of Monaco, with permission to build a castle there.

Having acquired from the monks of Saint-Pons and the consuls of Peille their private rights to part of the Rock ground, the Genoese took over the place and installed one of their consuls, Foulques de Castello, in June 1215, with three galleys and other ships to build a strong castle on the site still occupied by the Grimaldi palace.

Four towers were built: St. Mary's Tower, Middle Tower, Southern Tower and the Serravalle Tower, linked by a rampart. They encompass the Old Castle.

Another castle, called New Castle, was built some years later at the other end of the Rock to watch over the entrance to the port.

It was on the night of 8th January 1297 that Francis Grimaldi, known as Malizia, cunningly took possession of the Old Castle, which the Grimaldis left and repossessed depending on the vicissitudes of the wars between the Guelphs and Ghibellines until the sovereigns, and later on the princes of Monaco, settled in once and for all.

Over the next couple of centuries, the citadel underwent considerable changes.

Under Charles I, it took on the appearance of a fort,

Views of the Prince's Palace and Parade Ground, with the canons given by Louis XIV to the Prince of Monaco.

enlarged by Lambert with a new block featuring loggias between St. Mary's Tower and the Middle Tower.

During the siege of Monaco on the part of the Genoese between 1506-1507, the castle was severely damaged. Its long, laborious restoration which began during the reign of Lucien, who built the apartment known as Hercules apartment, was continued by Augustin, Stephen the Governor and Honoré I.

Augustin built the lookout tower to strengthen defence of the entrance and rearranged the living quarters on the occasion of Charles V's visit.

Stephen Grimaldi, tutor of Honoré I, entrusted the Milanese architect Domenico Gallo with restructuring the central courtyard: the large apartments' wing was completed by two porticoed galleries and the opposite wing was lifted by two floors and rested on a gallery bounded by large pillars.

Honoré I improved the defence system by means of a device that exploited the progress of artillery, divided up into two main buildings: the All-Saints Tower and the bastion of Serravalle, connected under-

ground.

It was Prince Honoré II who transformed the Castle into a Palace: the main entrance – that of the Small Quarters – was enlarged and decorated; in front of the courtyard of honour, facing the private apartments, the new Chapel of St. John the Baptist was built to replace the old oratory, and the large apartments' wing was extended. In the French style garden, laid out on the crag dominanting Fortveille, a bathing pavilion was built.

Honoré also enriched the art collections in the Palace. He furnished the rooms and reception rooms, which he had decorated with sumptuous tapestries.

His grandson Louis I continued along the same lines by building a dual revolving flight of steps in the courtyard of honour and opening the monumental gate in front of the Rock area.

Anthony I concentrated more on fortifications. He built the Oreillon Tower and restored the Serravalle bastion. To decorate the Palace, he used local artists such as Joseph Bressan and Augustin Vento.

During the French revolution, the Palace was sacked, looted and turned into a military barracks, before becoming a poorhouse.

When the Grimaldis were reinstated, the Palace was in such a shambles that Prince Honoré V was forced to have an entire wing demolished to extend the façade eastwards.

During the reigns of Prince Florestan and Prince Charles III, Princess Caroline had the façade that dominates the corner wing built and gardens laid out on the fortifications of the Serravalle bastion. In turn, Prince Albert I helped to improve the overall appearance of the Palace by building the Watch Tower pavilion whose rustic work is crowned by battlements reminiscent of the dynasty's Guelph origins.

Prince Rainier III ordered the restoration of the frescoes in the Gallery of Hercules.

On the site of the buildings demolished by Prince Honoré following on the sackings of the Revolution, he had a new wing built to house private apartments, as well as the Museum of Napoleonic Remembrance and archives.

Three pictures of the changing of the guard.

The changing of the guard – Everyday, before midday, a crowd of tourists gathers near the Palace to see the changing of the guard.

The police who come on duty leave the barracks at the opposite end of the square, preceded by fanfare, consisting of drums and trumpets, and goose-step towards the monumental entrance. The passing of orders takes place when the tower clock alongside St. Mary's tower strikes midday.

With the same ceremonial, the men coming off duty return to barracks.

After the changing of the guard two armed policemen remain on both sides of the monumental gate, crowned by the princes' coat-of-arms and inserted in its pediment.

Overview of the Court of Honour.

THE COURTYARD OF HONOUR

Beautifully proportioned and decorated in Italian Renaissance style, the Courtyard of Honour of the prince's Palace, previously planned by Domenico Gallo during the reign of Stephen the Governor, took on its present appearance under Prince Honoré II, who had the works supervised by the Genoese Giacomo and Taddeo Cantone, both architects and entrepreneurs. The Cantone brothers built the Chapel of St. John the Baptist and extended the south-western wing, known as the large apartments' wing, as far as the Serravalle bastion.

It was under the reign of Prince Louis I, grandson and successor of Honoré II, that the monumental gate was opened in the façade of the Palace looking over the square, known at the time as the Parade Ground, separating the Grimaldis' residence from the Rock area and the dual revolving flights of steps were built providing access to the Gallery of Hercules.

The present paving of the Courtyard of Honour, which was used to cover the 1700 cubic metres tank built during the mid- 16th century by Stephen Grimaldi, known as the Governor, to ensure a water supply during prolonged sieges, was built by order of Prince Rainier III in a ray design consisting of pebbles alternating with stone slabs.

In the Arms Gallery, crowned by the Gallery of Hercules, one can admire coaches belonging to Prince Charles III and Prince Albert I's station wagon used for hunting purposes.

On the ground floor of the opposite wing are the administrative offices, archives and library.

The Court of Honour overlooked the Gallery of Hercules to the right.

The elegant monumental flight of steps that leaves from the Court of Honour.

THE MONUMENTAL FLIGHT OF STEPS

If Prince Honoré's upbringing in Milanese territory under the wise guidance of Prince Federico Landi di Val di Taro and his marriage to an Italian noblewoman made him appreciate Florentine Renaissance masterpieces, Prince Louis I, grandson of Louis XIV – married to a countess known to the court of France, Charlotte Catherine, daughter of Marshal de Gramont – took Fontainbleau as his model when he decided to built a dual revolving flight of steps for the large apartments of the palace wing dominating Fontvieille.

Inspired by the famous horse-shoe flight of steps embelleshing Fontainebleau Palace, the architect had every one of the thirty steps of the two flights cut out of the same block of Carrara marble.

The balustrades are decorated with Portor marble spheres; the flight of steps is paved with Venetian mosaics in rosettes. The pillars are sculpted in high relief depicting prince's coats-of-arms and other war attributes.

Nowadays, in summer, the dual revolving flight of steps forms a wonderful background for the Philharmonic Orchestra of Monte Carlo during concerts conducted by the most famous conductors worlwide.

At the bottom of the Court of Honour the façade of the palatine Chapel of St. John the Baptist opens up.

Interior of the Chapel of St. John the Baptist.

On the following pages: 17th Century French School painting portraying the patron saint of Monaco Saint Dévote, the large stained-glass window with Saint Dévote in front of the judges by Nicolas Lorin, and the frescoed chapel dome.

THE CHURCH OF ST. JOHN THE BAPTIST

The foremost of the six parishes now forming the archdiocese of Monaco, the Chapel of St. John the Baptist was built by order of Prince Honoré III to replace the old oratory situated in the palace wing overlooking the Condamine, at the end of the passage leading from the door of the Small Quarters to the Courtyard of Honour.

On 15th October 1656, the Bishop of Nice came to bless the chapel built in the centre of the fourth wing of the Palace, in front of the Serravalle tower.

During the reign of Prince Charles III, the Chapel of St. John the Baptist was restored and so was its façade decorated by frescoes by Jacob Froshcle and Deschlerd'Augusbourg, depicting on the one side *scenes from the life of St. Dévote*, patron saint of the Principality, and on the other *episodes from the history of Monaco.*

During the same century, decorating of the interior was undertaken in Baroque style by the Roman artist and ceramist, Ernest Sprega (1829-1911), who was also charged with decorating the ceilings of the Palace dining-hall, not to mention the ceiling of the Hall of Mirrors.

A stained-glass window by Nicolas Lorin, master glazier of Chartres, depicts *Saint Dévote interrogated by judges.*

Two views of the Gallery of Hercules, with its decoration and Renaissance style arabesques.

THE GALLERY OF HERCULES

Built at the end of the Large Apartments' wing and above the Guards' Gallery, the Gallery of Hercules, which one enters by means of the dual revolving flight of steps from the Courtyard of Honour, dates back to the reign of Stephen the Governor who wanted to give the Grimaldi residence the majestic, harmonious look of Genoese palaces. It is by the Milanese architect Domenico Gallo.

Consisting of round arches resting on colums, it is bound by a white marble balustrade and outshines the massive, austere wing in front of it.

The gallery vaults are frescoed with patterns reminiscent of Italian Renaissance leitmotifs while in the fourteen lunettes, episodes narrate *the childhood, toils and death of Hercules.*

These frescoes were painted by the Genoese artist Orazio Ferrari, who Prince Honoré II called to the Palace to do various decorations; he likewise instructed him to paint scenes and organise balls, ballets and other shows provided for the entertainment of illustrious guests. They have been restored several times, changing their original nature in places.

That is why Prince Rainier III gave up the idea of touching them up and opted for changing the wall

A detail of the decoration of the Court of Honour, with the 16th Century frescoes by Luca Cambiaso.

A detail of the Renaissance frescoes of the Gallery of Hercules.

Two details of the frescoes in the vault of the Gallery of Hercules, in Italian Renaissance style.

decoration and applying four frescoes by Pier Francesco Mazzucchelli, known as Il Morazzone (1573-1626), an artist of the Caravaggian school.

Mazzucchelli's compositions alternate with Renaissance decorative panels depicting mythological or legendary celebrities: *Antiope, Semiramis, Artemisia and Sphiron.*

The Gallery of Hercules is particularly dear to the Monacans. In fact, it is here that the sovereign appears during important events while onlookers gather in the Courtyard of honour.

For instace, for the traditional swearing-in ceremony or the presentation of a future princess or new-born prince.

The north-east façade of the Courtyard of Honour was decorated by the Genoese artist Luca Cambiaso (1527-1585) under Prince Honoré I. Along the two overlapping friezes in the cartouches, *mythological scenes* alternate with *episodes of Greek and Roman history.*

Two pictures of the Gallery of Mirrors.

THE GALLERY OF MIRRORS

The Gallery of Mirrors, perpendicular to the Gallery of Hercules, acts as an antechamber to the large apartments' wing. It is here that the Prince's guests wait to be received by the Royal Family at receptions, especially at those held in the Throne Room.

This gallery gets its name from the mirrors placed on both walls, creating an optical illusion.

The gold and white decoration, lit by light from the large windows and chandeliers embellished by crystal drops, enhances the glitter of the marble mosaics on the floor.

Among the other ornaments decorating the gallery, it is worth mentioning the Ming vases, Japanese cups and busts of *Prince Charles III*, sculpted by Mathieu Mesnier, *Prince Albert I* and *Princess Alice* by Fabio Stecchi, and *Prince Louis II* by Louis Maubert, placed on marble bases.

On the opposite side to this series of princes' busts, visitors can admire the *Nymphe Salmacis*, one of the most famous works by the Monacan artist Joseph-François Bosio (1768-1845), official sculptor to Napoleon I, Louis XVIII and Charles X and author of the quadriga crowning the Arc de Triomphe of the Carrousel in Paris.

Another perspective of the Gallery of Mirrors.

Prince Rainier III, Princess Grace and their three children depicted in the large painting by Ralph Wolfe Cowan, at the bottom of the Gallery of Mirrors.

When in 1961 he created the International Monte Carlo Television Festival "to favour exceptional contributions to information and the entertainment of people worldwide through television programmes of artistic merit and remarkable talent", Prince Rainier III decide to make copies of the Nymphe Salmacis on a reduced scale as trophies.

At the bottom of the gallery, a large painting by Ralph Wolfe Cowan protrays *Prince Rainier III, Princess Grace and their three children.*

A view of the York Room.

THE BALL ROOM AND YORK ROOM

Prince Honoré III, who often resided in Paris and on his Torigni estate in Lower Normandy, left the responsibility of Monacan administration to Chevalier de Grimaldi, the governor general previously appointed by his father James I and reconfirmed to his office after the latter's abdication. Naturally this did not stop him from returning regularly to Monaco to check how the country was doing in person.

During the summer of 1767, he had been staying at the Palace for some weeks when Prince Edward Augustus, the Duke of York, was brought to the castle; he had suddenly fallen ill while sailing from Genoa to Marseilles.

Even though he was treated by doctors from Nice, he died some days later on 17th September.

In the room where he stayed, turned into a funeral chamber, last respects were paid to his corpse, which was then escorted with full pomp and ceremony to the ship that was to take him back to Great Britain.

Touched by the care taken of his brother in the Palace, King George III of England invited Prince Honoré III to London and gave him a very warm welcome.

This historical event gave rise to a legend according to which, while the Duke of York was dying, a woman

A corner of the luxurious Duke of York room.

On the following pages: a detail of the canopy and alcove ceiling in the York room and the bed where the brother of George III of England died on 17th September 1767.

dressed in white with her gaze turned towards the Grimaldi Palace appeared at the tip of Vigie, a small promontory on the Roquebrune cost. When the ship carrying the corpse of the Duke of York disappeared behind the Rock, the woman threw herself into the sea with a desperate cry.

Since then the room in which the Duke died has been known as the York room.

As a royal bedroom, it had already been sumptuously decorated at the time of Prince Anthony I, and this is why it was called the *Gilt Alcove room*.

Richly furnished and decorated with magnificent ceramics, the Antechamber of York, likewise known as the Red Room, houses paintings of historic and artistic interest: the *portraits of Armand Charles de La Porte*, Duke of Meilleraye; *Jeromy Grimaldi*, Bishop of Aix-en-Provence, painted by Egmont; *Cardinal Mazarin*, by Nicolas Mignard; two large landscapes, the *River Banks* and *Castle Entrance*, attributed to the school of Jacques Van Arthois, and views of the Principality in 1815, signed by the German artist L. Peters.

A bronze by Coutan, offered by the people of Monaco to Prince Albert I on the occasion of his appointment as Fellow of the Royal Society of France,

On these pages, some examples of the magnificent furnishings of the York Room: a three-winged piece of furniture in Chinese lacquer with mirror and candelabras in gilded bronze, a close-up of a putto supporting a candelabrum, the Louis XIV door decorations and a close-up of a piece of furniture in ebony with a vase of flowers encrusted with polychrome hard stones.

On the ceiling of the York Room Gregorio de Ferrari (1644-1726) portrayed fame in the centre and the allegories of Autumn and Summer in the lunettes.

portrays *Fame on horseback*.

Florentine majolicas and hunting plates by Moustiers with the Grimaldi coat-of-arms complete the decoration.

In the York room, marbles, paintings, sumptuous tapestries, the large bed in sculpted, gilt wood, the balustrade and frame of the alcove, the Louis XIV style ebony furniture inlaid with hard stones or decorated with lacquered panels of Chinese origin, and a large Boulle clock with two candelabras are clearly reminiscent of the elegance and refinement of rooms in the Palace of Versailles.

The vault frescoes, partially restored during the 19th century, feature figurative art by Gregorio De Ferrari, a Genoese artist (1644-1726) and architectural perspectives by Alexandre Haffner of Bologna.

The central figure portrays *Fame* and bears the coat-of-arms of the Grimaldis.

In the lunettes, allegorical figures evoke the four seasons of the year. In each of the corners, decorative patterns bear the interlaced initials of Prince Anthony I and his wife, Princess Marie de Lorraine.

Above the alcove, we can admire Juno, protectress of marriages and births.

Numerous portraits are hung on the walls of the York room, including those of Prince Anthony I by

A detail of the painted ceiling in the alcove of the York Room.

The Education of Love, painted by Louis Lagrenee (1725-1805).

Hyacinthe Rigaud, Louis I by François de Troy, and his wife, Charlotte de Gramont, by Sebastien Bourdon, Countess Saint Géran and Mademoiselle de Chateua-Thiers, by Pierre Mignard, and Princess Catherine de Brignole-Sale, wife of Prince Honoré III.

The floor of the room is in marble mosaic-work, decorated in the four corners with the coats of arms of the Princes of Monaco.

The York room is kept for royal guests and heads of State received at the Palace.

A Boulle pendulum with circular movement displayed above a fire-place in the Yellow Room.

A corner of the Yellow Room or Louis XV Room.

The elegant fire place crowned by the high mirror in the Louis XV Room.

THE YELLOW ROOM

A Chinese lacquer cabinet, a chest of drawers in precious walnut enriched with chiselled bronze patterns and a Moustiers ceramic plate with the Grimaldi coat of arms decorate the Yellow Room, also known as the Louis XV Room.

The walls are hung with *portraits* of *Jacques Matignon*, who took over the Grimaldi name when marrying the crown princess Louise Hippolyte, by Nicolas Largillière and *Princess Louise Hippolyte*, painted in Monaco in 1712 by Jean-Baptiste van Loo.

A canvas by Hyacinthe Rigaud portrays *Françoise de Bourbon known as Mademoiselle de Blois*, daughter of Louis XIV and Madame Montespan, resembling Diane goddess of the hunt, while another by Nicolas Largillière depicts *Louise Bourbon known as Mademoiselle de Nantes.*

The two ornamental panels over the door are by Hohé, an artist from Munich; they are reminiscent of typical Bavarian Alp landscapes where stags and fawns run wild. Over the hearth, a gilt Louis XV and a Boulle clock with a circular movement can be admired.

Portrait of the Princess of Monaco Louise Hippolyte by J.B. van Loo.

A corner of the beautiful Louis XV Room, also known as the Terrace Room.

THE LOUIS XV ROOM

The Yellow Room and Louis XV Room form an apartment reserved for important lady guests.

The Louis XV Room, likewise known as the Terrace Room, was decorated during the second half of the 18th Century. The tapestries in Alsatian printed material, Pompadour pink armchairs, shaped furniture, a mirror with Marie de Lorraine's initials and rare ornaments make the surroundings both elegant and cosy.

Two paintings of mythological scenes – *The Toilette of Venus* by François Lemoyne and *The Education of Love* by Jean François Lagrenée, a pupil of Boucher – blend in with the style of the room.

Two other paintings are worthy of note: *Love in meditation*, attributed to Bartolomeo Schidone, and *Mary Magdalene* by the Roman artist Domenico Feti. Two ornamental panels over the doors, painted by Hohé, depict the *Moulins district* of Monte Carlo.

Right throughout history, the sovereigns and princes of Monaco have shown considerable interest in the arts and encouraged patronage. When the main concern of heads of royal families was the defense of strong fortresses, Honoré I had his palace decorated with paintings by well-known artists. Later on, Honoré II housed considerable collections in the palace. Apart from pieces of gold-work, Gobelin tapestries, valuable furniture and rare porcelain, inventories reveal the presence of over seven hundred paintings, signed by the greatest Renaissance artists. Princes Louis I and Anthony I helped to enrich this heritage, which unfortunately went missing or was destroyed or sacked during the revolution.

Prince Anthony I invited famous artists to the palace. One of them, Jean Baptiste van Loo (1684-1745), who belonged to a family of French artists of Dutch descent painted several portraits of the Grimaldi family, including the one on page 44 portraying *Princess Louis Hippolyte* and, in the background, part of the Rock and prince's Palace.

The "Polish" bed in the Louis XV Room.

18th Century pendulum "of the Three Graces".

The Parade Ground of Monaco in 1732 in a painting by Joseph Bressan.

A corner of the Officer's Room, with the interesting Florentine Francis I cabinet against a wall.

THE OFFICERS' ROOM

During important official receptions, the Prince's guests summoned to the Gallery of Mirrors are received by the guards of honour in the Officers' Room.

In this sumptuously decorated room full of frescoes, two Francis I Florentine cabinets in sculpted, painted and inlaid wood blend the charm of their harmonious lines with the mysteries of their numerous secret drawers, so dear to Renaissance gentlefolk.

Magnificent paintings adorn the walls, some of which are noteworthy on account of their artistic value, such as *The Harvest* by Jacques Van Arthois, *Dry Dock*, a 17th Century Flemish landscape attributed to Giullaume van de Velde by certain art critics and to Abram Stork by others, not to mention a *portrait of the Duchess of Aumont-Mazarin* by Marie Verroust.

Two works of art in the Officers' Room are worth mentioning on account of their documentary interest: *Monaco Palace*, seen in perspective from the Parade Ground (now Palace Square) and the *Parade Ground during a parade.*

Thanks to the minute drawing, these two paintings by the Monacan artist Dominique Joseph Bressan reveal that the Grimaldi palace, Palace Square and Rock area, with St. Barbara's Chapel in the foreground, have not changed in appearance since 1732.

Together with his compatriots Jean Augustin Vento and Horace Sigaldi, Dominique Joseph Bressan formed part of a group of artists commissioned by Prince Anthony I to do original paintings or copies of paintings by more famous artists.

The three arches that divide the Blue Room, or Louis XV Room, in two.

A Louis XV gilt wooden console crowned by a majestic mirror in the Blue Room.

THE LOUIS XV ROOM

The Louis XV Room or Blue room, that precedes the Throne Room, is divided into two parts by three arches and covered by a ceiling decorated with frescoes in Pompeian style.

The works of art displayed on the large shelves, such as Delft ceramic plates and Sèvres blue vases, are enhanced by the light reflected by the huge Venetian glass chandeliers.

Two official portraits portray *Louis XV* and *Marie Leszczynska* respectively and are by François Stiémart; they are copies of the originals by Jean Baptiste van Loo who supervised their execution, and were offered to Prince Anthony I by King Louis XV. Nearby are children's portraits: *Charlotte Grimaldi* known as Mademoiselle de Valentinois and, later on, Mademoiselle de Monaco, daughter of Princess Louise Hippolyte and *Honoré Grimaldi*, Marquis des Baux, the future Prince Honoré III. These children's portraits are by Pierre Gobert. Two 18th Century paintings of the French school, *Spring* and *Autumn*, a painting by Annibale Carrache, *Polyphemus and Galatea*, and a *Turkish Combat* by Jacques Courtois, known as the Borgogne, complete the rich decoration of the Blue Room.

Overview and close-up of the Throne Room.

THE THRONE-ROOM

The old state room also known as the Grimaldi Room, and now called the Throne Room, has been the setting for official Monacan Court events since the 16th Century.

In this room, when a new sovereign comes to the throne, high-ranking dignitaries and government and municipal officials swear allegiance to the Prince. In this room, on the 18th April 1956 the civil marriage between H.R.H. Prince Rainier III and Grace Patricia Kelly was celebrated by the Prince Minister.

Every year, the day before the National Holiday celebrated on 19th November, the Royal Family receives in this room religious, civil and military authorities, not to mention representatives of the consular corps accredited in Monaco, at a reception in honour of decorated and promoted members of the princely Orders of St. Charles and Grimaldi.

On the walls of the Throne Room, tapestries in red silk damask alternate with gilt wooden panels. The ceiling is frescoed while the floor is in marble mosaic-work.

The lacquered gilt throne in Empire style, placed on a dais, is crowned by a sumptuous canopy in Vienna velvet embroidered in gold thread, on which the prince's crown rests.

The back of the throne is decorated with the mono-

DEO JUVANTE

QVI DICIT SE NOSSE DEVM
ET MANDATA EIVS NON
CVSTODIT MENDAX
EST

The majestic Renaissance fire-place in the Throne Room.

The family of the Duke de Valentinois, painted between 1733 and 1734 by Pierre Gobert.

gram of Prince Charles III. Above the throne and in the centre of the canopy is the coat of arms of the house of Grimaldi, according to a cartoon dating back to before the foundation of the Order of St. Charles.

In front of the throne, a large Renaissance style Turbie stone bears the inscription: "Qui dicit se nosse deum et mandata ejus non custodit, mendax est".

On the wall of the room in front of the windows, a large painting done by Pierre Gobert in 1733 portrays *the family of the Duke and Duchess of Valentinois*, Jacques and Louise Hippolyte Grimaldi.

The boy with the gold cloth suit embroidered in silver to the extreme eight of the painting is the future Prince Honoré III; from left to right, his brothers and sisters: Marie Charles Auguste, known as Count of Carladez and later Count of Matigon, before becoming brigadier of the Forest regiment; François Charles Madeleine Joseph, Count of Torigny, who then became officer in the King's Infantry regiment; Louise Françoise Thérèse, called Mademoiselle d'Estouteville and later on Mademoiselle de Valentinois; Charlotte, known as Mademoiselle de Valentinois and later on Mademoiselle de Monaco, and Charles Maurice known under the name of Chevalier of Monaco who was later injured during the Battle of Fontenoy.

Other official portraits of the dynasty decorate the walls of the Throne Room: *Prince Honoré III* by Louis Tocqué, *Princess Caroline* by Marie Verroust,

Ceiling of the Throne Room: the 17th Century frescoes portray the signs of the zodiac and another detail with the history of Alexander the Great.

Prince Charles III by François Biard, *Prince Albert I*, by Léon Bonnat (1833-1922) who painted a famous portrait of Victor Hugo, *Prince Louis II*, in the general's uniform of the French army, Philip de Lazlo de Lombos (1869-1937) and *Princess Charlotte* by the same artist.

The *ceiling frescoes* by Orazio Ferrari were restored in 1863 by the Monacan artist Philibert Florence (1839-1918). On the pendentives, one can see the *signs of the zodiac* and on the vault an *episode from the history of Alexander the Great*.

Above the interleading doors, coats of arms of families related to the Grimaldi are portrayed.

On both sides of the canopy above the throne, mobile panels conceal openings providing access to the rooms that house musicians during receptions.

A beautiful 17th Century painted panel lines the walls of the Mazarin Room.

The majestic portrait of Princess Grace, painted by Ricardo Macaron in 1974.

THE MAZARIN ROOM

Prince Honoré IV, born in 1758 and son of Honoré III and Marie Catherine de Brignole-Sale, married in 1777 Louise Félicité Victoire d'Aumont, the only daughter of Louis Marie Gui d'Aumont and Louise Jeanne de Durfort, Duchess of Mazarin.

Louise Félicité had inherited the duchy of Mazarin, the principality of Château Porcien, the county of Fère and Marle, the counties of Belfort, Ferrette, Thann and Rosemont, the barony of Altkirche, the seigniories of Delle and Isenheim, the marquisate of Chilly, the county of Longjumeau and the marquisate of Guiscard.

This sumptuous room, reminiscent of the Grimaldis union with the Aumont-Mazarino, is covered in multicoloured panelling painted by 17th Century Italian artists, including a 17th Century *portrait of Cardinal Mazarin* of the French school and two scenes inspired by the *life of Hercules.*

The ceiling frescoes are inspired by the arabesques in the panelling and, in the corners, they alternate the coats of arms of the house of Grimaldi and the Duchess d'Aumont Mazarin.

The Boulle furniture includes a magnificent writing-desk and chest of drawers. The display cabinets are full of objects from the collections of Prince Louis II: ceramics, surgical instruments and Provençal manger figurines.

Near the hearth, on an easel, one can admire a majestic *portrait of Princess Grace*, painted in 1974 by Ricardo Macaron.

In the Matignon antechamber, a painting by the Provençal artist Bernardin Mimault portrays *Jeanne Grimaldi*, Countess Trivulce and sister of Honoré II, dressed as a penitent.

The portrait of Cardinal Mazarin in the medallion above the fire-place and a Boulle chest-of-drawers crowned by a panel depicting Hercules killing the Hydra.

CHAMBRE LOUIS XIII

The Mazarin Room leads into the Louis XIII Room through a magnificent 17th Century painted wooden door.

The Louis XIII room.

THE LOUIS XIII ROOM

The Mazarin Room leads into the Louis XIII Room also known as the Marble Alcove Room, whose austerity is attributed to the exceptional quality of certain paintings on display.

Among the paintings three portraits must be pointed out: a *profile of Lucian I*, sovereign of Monaco from 1503 to 1523, attributed to Giovanni Ambrogio de Predis (1455 ca.-1508 ca.), pupil of Leonardo da Vinci; *Prince Honoré II* by Philippe de Champaigne (1602-1674), and *Prince Hercules*, son of Prince Honoré II, by a 17th Century artist of the French school. But the master-pieces in the Louis XIII Room are without a doubt *The Music Lesson* and *The Embroideress*.

The Music Lesson was attributed both to Giorgione and Titian, but contemporary critics are more inclined to believe the second hypothesis.

Experts cannot reach an agreement on the painter of The Embroideress; some think it is Holbein, others W. Scrots, the official artist of the Court of Mary of Hungary, sister of Emperor Charles V.

The *Slave with a dog* by Luca Giordano, Neapolitan Baroque artist (1634-1705), completes the picture, enhanced by the furniture in the room, in particular by the large four-poster bed in an alcove bounded by a Portor marble balustrade.

When visiting Monaco, Cardinal Angelo Roncalli, the future Pope John XXIII, stayed in this room.

Close-up of the 17th Century painted panel and a Boulle writing-desk.

Partial view of the Louis XIII room.

An imposing ceramic produced in Monaco by E. Strega in 1881.

A view of the swimming-pool in the Palace's private gardens.

THE PALACE GARDENS

When the fortress was turned into a Palace, the Princes of Monaco wanted to create green parks near the defence structures which still remained indispensable for the safeguarding of the country.

At the foot of the large apartments' wing, on both sides of the Bay of Fonteveille, Prince Honoré II had a large terrace laid out with rectilinear avenues featuring orange and bitter orange trees. Three white marble fountains by Martino Solaro liven up the flower-beds, and, on the Serravalle side, a building known as the baths pavilion featuring swimming-pools, tanks, rest-rooms and terraces decorated with statues also by Solaro offered guests of the royal family the pleasures of a holiday resort.

During the sad years of the revolution, the gardens were broken up, sold or made available to the military authorities.

After the restoration, the private apartments' wing and baths pavilion had to be demolished because of their poor state of repair.

In the parts where it was destroyed, Princess Caroline, wife of Prince Florestan I, relaid the gardens, whose original charm were restored by Prince Rainier and Princess Grace tastefully, harmoniously and with natural charm. At the bottom, on the cliff terrace, Prince Rainier III set up a Zoological Acclimatization Centre that recreates the environmental conditions of tropical fauna.

A partial view of a room in the Napoleonic Remembrance Museum, in the wing of the Palace recently restructured by Prince Rainier III.

The bust of Napoleon I by Antonio Canova.

THE NAPOLEONIC MUSEUM AND ARCHIVES MUSEUM

Prince Louis II loved collecting objets d'art, unusual bindings, beautiful ceramics and medals.

He was particularly interested in the Napoleonic era.

The countless souvenirs that he collected from this period, which was both glorious and tragic at the same time for French history, form a valuable collection which Prince Rainier III wanted to make accessible to the public by creating, in the recently rebuilt wing of the Palace, the Museum of Napoleonic Remembrance featuring heraldic devices, flags, imperial eagles and objects that belonged to the Emperor such as the head-gear that he wore to the Battle of Marengo.

The most noteworthy pieces in the collection are the *bust of Napoleon I* by Antonio Canova, a snuff-box left by the Emperor to the great-grandmother of Prince Louis II, a swatch of the cloak that Napoleon wore the day in which he was crowned Emperor by Pope Pius VII at Notre Dame in Paris, his memoirs of St. Helena, and the games and shoes of his son called Aiglon.

The Archives Museum of the prince's Palace, which leads into the Museum of Napoleonic Remembrance, displays some treasures kept in the various collections of the Palace as from the age of Prince Charles III: archives of the government, court-houses, the old Commune, religious institutes,

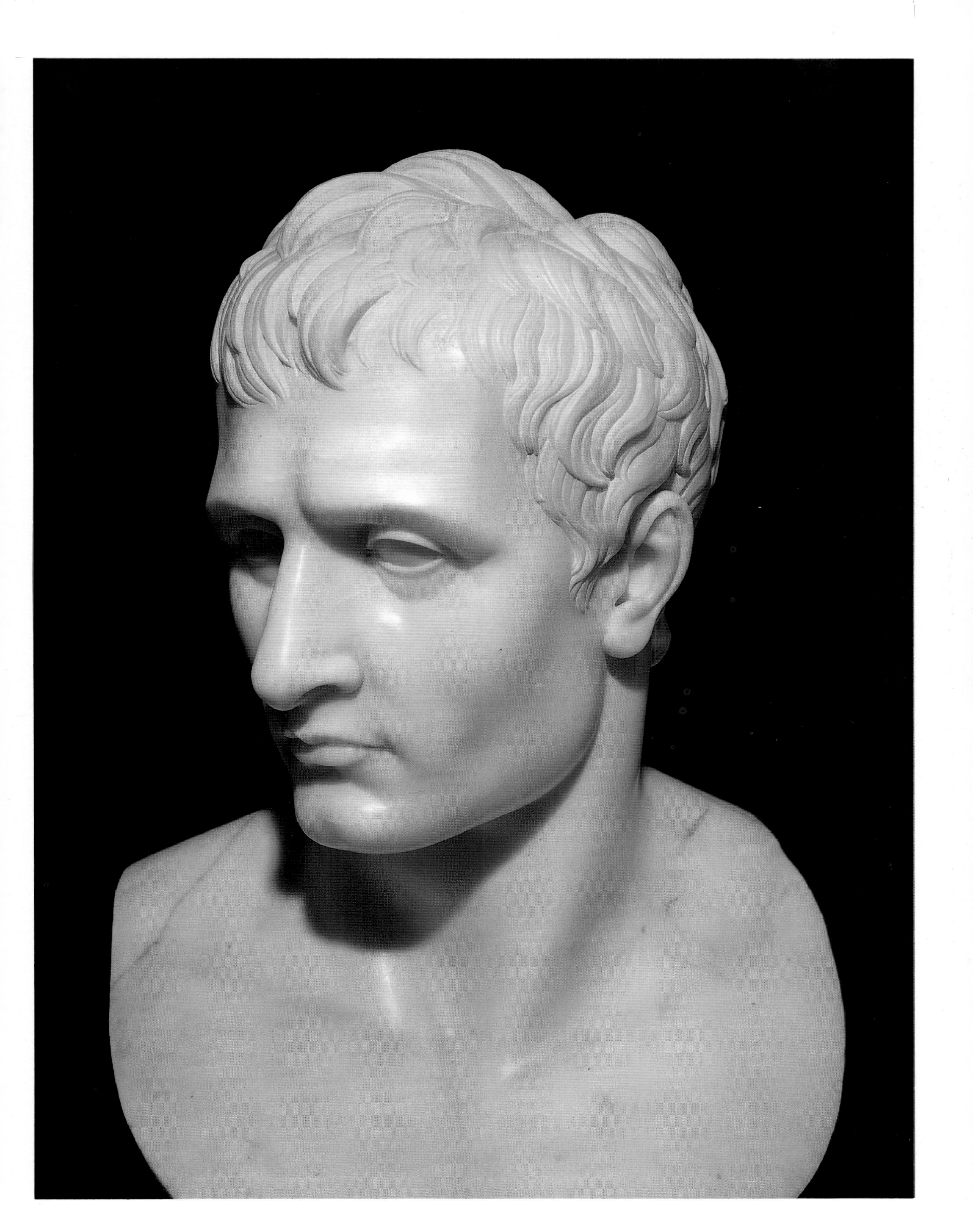

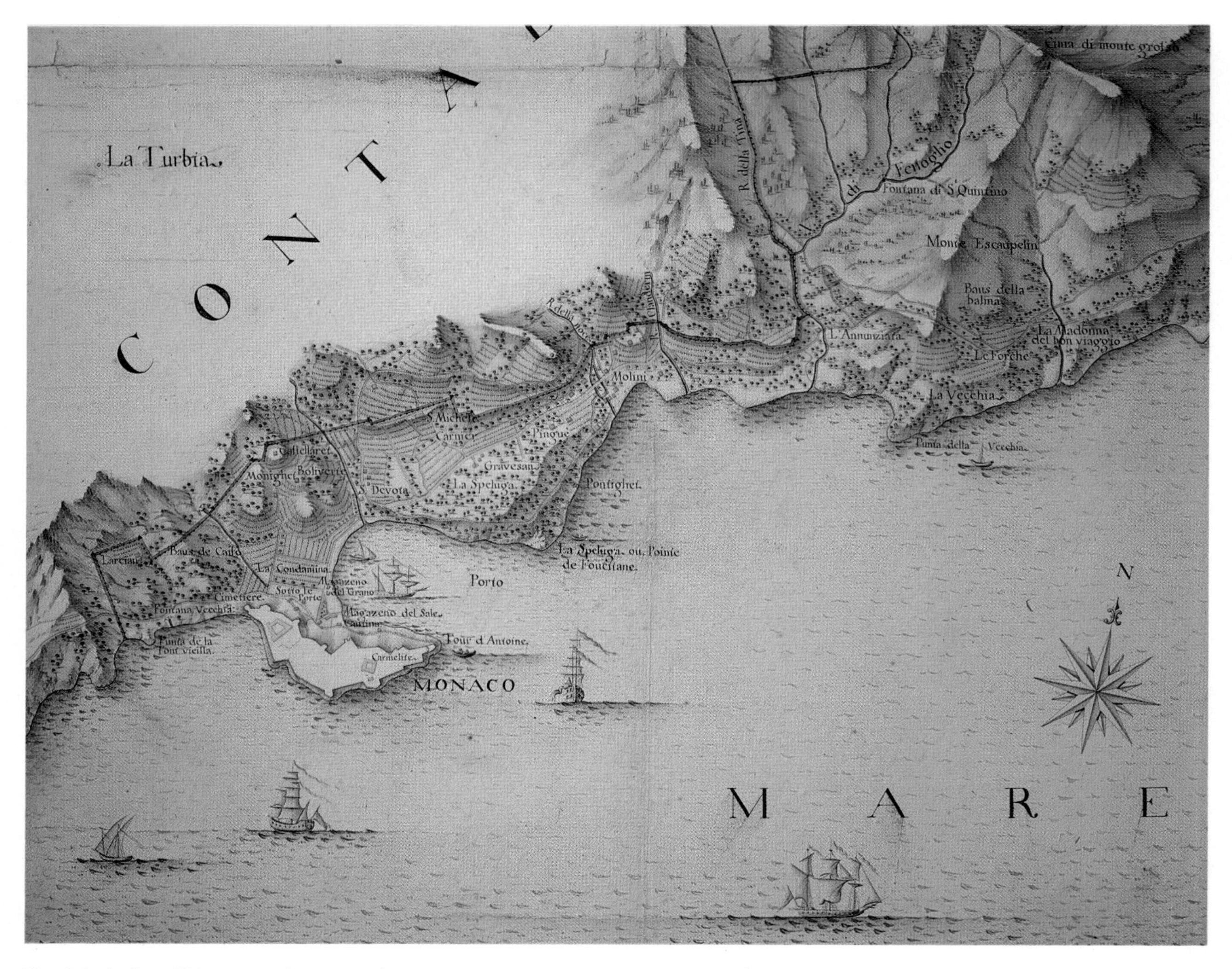

The Principality of Monaco as it appeared on a late-18th Century map.

notary's offices and all the valuable documents that the Monacan descendents of the Matignon sovereigns and Dukes d'Aumont-Mazarin managed to salvage in their Parisian residences at the time of the revolution.

The official correspondence of Monacan sovereigns and Princes, not to mention their personal correspondence, are a limitless source of information for researchers like, for instance, a missive from Charles V thanking Augustine I for offering his help at the Battle of Pavia, or some letters from Prince Anthony I to Cardinal Fleury, Marshal de Berwick or Destouches, Director of the Opera House in Paris.

In the Matignon collection, fourteen out of the thirty-nine known letters from Michel Eyquem de Montaigne are kept, and so are forty letters from Francis I and a dozen or so from Marguerite d'Angoulême, not to mention letters from King Henry III, King Henry IV, Catherine de Medici and Marguerite de Valois.

Apart from great names in history, Cromwell, Napoleon I, and Napoleon III, great names in literature also feature: Bossuet, Lamartine, Renan and Colette. Art is represented by Largillière, Lancret and Bonnat and music by Couperin, Sant Saën and Massenet.

The Palace Archives publish a magazine entitled "Annáles monégasques" that basically aims at "giving national and foreign history researchers, the chance to get to know the object of their studies and patient work".

The exterior of the National Fine Arts Museum by Charles Garnier.

THE NATIONAL FINE ARTS MUSEUM

The National Fine Arts Museum is set in the elegant setting of Villa Sauber, one of the latest examples of eclectic architecture in Monte Carlo, built by Charles Garnier in the Portier district.

The avenues of the garden are decorated with sculptures and rose-gardens. They are works by the great artists at the time: Jean Baptiste Carpeaux, Antoine Bourdelle, Gustave Pimienta, Aristide Maillol and Emma de Sigaldi, a Monacan artist, whose works abound in the Principality.

Together with an 18th Century *Neapolitan crèche*, Villa Sauber houses rich *collections* of 19th Century *automatons* and 18th and 19th Century *dolls*, collected by Madeleine de Galéa and offered by her grandson Christian de Galéa to the Principality of Monaco; moreover, it presents current fashion trends on the part of Parisian haute couture designers.

The National Fine Arts Museum displays approximately ninety automatons.

Some of them are famous collectors' pieces: *The*

Two pictures of the Snake Charmer of 1890, one of the finest pieces in the Museum.

Other examples of the collection of automatons: the Dining Room of 1885 and "At the home of Alfred de Musset" of 1860.

Lawyer who gesticulates wildly; the *Artist painter*, who shuts his eyes for some time before starting to draw in his sketch-book and then proudly presents his work of art; *Pierrot with dogs*, in the circus games tradition; *Pierrot the writer*, who turns up the flame of his oil burner to throw light on the letter he is writing to Columbine; *The snake charmer*, with a bewitching expression on her face, and a whole series of virtuoso players.

Almost all the automatons in the Museum are equipped with a musical mechanism, which is usually driven by the main motor, resulting from clockwork movements.

One of the most interesting show-cases contains the various pieces needed to build automatons, which usually took about twenty artisans. As many of these trades have since disappeared, modern restorers must be familiar with these techniques in order to use them if need be.

The little dolls' world, reminiscent of childhood dreams and heroines of fantastic novels, documents the costumes, games, customs and trades of once upon a time. Displayed among décor built to scale, the dolls, perhaps better than any other form of artistic expression, evoke scenes of a past which would like to continue to exist.

The impressive exterior of the Oceanographic Museum, which looms up out of the sea.

THE OCEANOGRAPHIC MUSEUM

Built between 1899 and 1910 – its opening date – to house collections of underwater species brought back by Prince Albert I from his expeditions and scientific campaigns, especially from the Azores and Spitzberg, the Oceanographic Museum offers visitors an overview of sea sciences and techniques.

Connected to the Oceanographic Institute, which was also founded by Prince Albert I in Paris, the Oceanographic Museum is fitted out with laboratories where specialists of all nationalities conduct research together with the "International Laboratory of Marine Radioactivity", a scientific institution founded in Monaco following on a three-party agreement between the International Atomic Energy Agency, Oceanographic Institute and Monacan Governement.

The Oceanographic Museum possesses a rich library specialized in marine sciences, an endless mine of information for researchers who come to consult it on the spot or correspond with its services.

The Museum, which seems to rise straight out of the Mediterranean, was built in Neoclassic style. Its imposing façade is decorated with majestic sulptures by Gustave Dussart (1875-1952).

Very close to the Oceanographic Museum, at the viewpoint called "Le Rondeau", in the Saint Martin gardens overhanging the steep cliff-face of the Rock, a statue portrays Prince Albert I wearing a hooded overcoat at the helm of his ship; it was erected in 1951.

This bronze statue on a marble base by François Cogné, member of the French Institute, was inaugurated by Prince Rainier III on the 11th April 1951, the day of the national holiday([1]).

On that occasion, the Polygraphic Institute of Monaco published the fourth edition of the "Career of a Navigator", a book of memoirs in which Prince Albert I narrates his initial experiences as a seaman at the service of oceanographic science. The book, with a preface by Professor Paul Portier, was illustrated by the Monacan artist and engraver of Catalan origin, Luis V. Molné.

The fifth edition of the book, with an introduction by Commander Jacques Yves Cousteau and a preface by Commander Jules Rouch, was published in 1966 on the occasion of the 1st International Congress on the History of Oceanography, held at the Oceanographic Museum under the patronage of Prince Rainier III.

([1]) The following year, the national holiday was changed from 11th April to 19th November.

The bronze statue of Prince Albert I, founder of the Museum, displayed in the St. Martin Gardens.

The Conference Room inside the Oceanographic Museum.

Thanks to the Argos system, established by Ifremer in 1986, it was possible to study in-depth the migrations of turtles across the Atlantic.

The Conference Room of the Oceanographic Museum – The Conference Room of the Oceanographic Museum has been the setting for great international scientific meetings.

Just before it was revamped, it was used for an air experiment; in fact, in this room the French engineer, Léger, experimented the maiden flight of a helicopter with one passenger on board, Dr. Jules Richard, faithful companion of Prince Albert I's scientific expeditions and Director of the Oceanographic Museum, who agreed to be literally tied to the craft for this few metre ascent world première.

In this same room, in 1959, Prince Rainier III let out the first cry of alarm against the danger of atomic waste that threatens underwater life. In 1966, in this same room, the 1st International Congress on the History of Oceanography was held.

Among the illustrious guests present, mention must be made of the President of the Republic of Senegal, Léopold Sédar Senghor, member of the Academy of France and winner of the Prince Peter of Monaco prize in 1977; when handed the prize, he gave the Oceanographic Museum a conference on the origins of man.

Nowadays countless visitors flock to this room to see documentaries on sea life.

EX. 1

A view of the Aquarium.

Exotic acquatic plants in the Aquarium of the Oceanograhic Museum and two views of the glass-cases.

The Aquarium – The Aquarium of the Oceanographic Museum is no doubt one of the most famous of its kind in the world. Over eight tanks, in which for every species the original natural envinronment is recreated with minerals and local flora, contain fishes of all shapes and colours from the Mediterranean, Red Sea, Atlantic, Indian Ocean and Pacific, not to mention shell-fish, giant squid, turtles and other species of pelagic fauna.

The tanks are filled with sea water pumped directly to the foot of the Museum and renewed incessantly.

They were designed according to the avant-garde techniques of the study of plant and animal life in an acquarium; it is worth emphasizing that the 1st International Congress on this new science was held at the Oceanographic Museum in 1960.

The Scientific Rooms – The actual museum is housed on two floors.

On the ground floor, a statue by Denys Puech portrays Prince Albert I at the helm.

On the one side is the conference room which we mentioned earlier and on the other the collections room featuring deep sea fishing equipment, embalmed animals and skeletons of bears, sperm whales, dolphins and other types of whales.

On the first floor is a reconstruction of Prince Albert I's laboratory on his yacht, the Princess Alice II.

The Princess Alice II, Prince Albert I's last yachts, was 73,15 metres long. With a tonnage of 1420, it could reach speeds of 13 knots.

It was in this laboratory of the Princess Alice II that

Overview of the Applied Oceanography Room.

Professor Charles Richet, Nobel Prize-winner for physics in 1913, and Professor Paul Portier, member of the Institute of France, discovered the phenomenon of anaphylaxis, revealing that physalies siphonophores, classed as jelly fish, manage to immobilize their prey as soon as they touch it thanks to a poison secreted.

Contrary to its vaccination, the anaphylactic phenomenon increases the organism's sensitivity to poison when an initial dose of this poison is injected into the organism.

The discovery of Professors Richet and Portier is at the root of further progress made by researchers in the field of immunotherapy.

In the eastern wing of the first floor, about ten thousand species of shells are exhibited and catalogued. One can also admire a rich collection of handicrafts made with marine flora and fauna.

Penguins, elephants, sea-lions and polar birds embalmed and arranged amid décor reminiscent of ice-flows create the impression of real Arctic surroundings.

In the opposite wing, on the same floor, one can feast one's eyes on instruments and measuring instruments mainly invented, manufactured and utilized by oceanographic pioneers, among whom Prince Albert I excelled; in fact, Emile Bertin defined him as "the founder".

Countless paintings adorn the walls of the Oceanographic Museum, mainly by the French artist, Louis Tinayre (1861-1942), who accompanied Prince Albert I in some of his expeditions and painted fishing and hunting scenes live during expeditions.

The third edition of Prince Albert I's memoirs "A

The Zoological Oceanography Room displays skeletons of great marine mammals, such as whales, killer-whales, narwhals, etc.

Navigator's Career", published in 1914, is illustrated with 150 drawings by Tinayre.

As from 1st January 1911, a weather station was annexed to the Oceanographic Museum. It was operative until 1960 when it was replaced by the Scientific Centre, an organism created by Prince Rainier III for the study and measurement of radioactivity in the air and meteoric water, the dating – using carbon 14 – of fossilized living beings, the fluctuation of marine radioactivity, plancton and algae, and polluting effects on the sea caused by underwater fall-out, seismic phenomena, medical application of radioisotopes, microbiology, etc.

Other scientific activities in the marine sector – Apart from the aforementioned Oceonographic Museum, Scientific Centre and International Marine Radioactivity Laboratory, other scientific istitutes concentrate on the marine sector, in particular the International Hydrographic Organisation, an intergovernmental body that aims at coordinating the hydrographic services of member states, and the Monacan Association for the Protection of Nature, charged with developing and managing Monaco's Underwater Reserve, created by Prince Rainier III to protect and re-establish the marine flora and fauna.

Founded by Prince Albert I and at present chaired by Prince Rainier III, the International Commission for the Scientific Exploration of the Mediterranean Sea, which boasts seventeen member countries along the Mediterranean coast, collaborates with the Intergovernmental Oceonographic Commission and the International Fishing Council of the F.A.O. in studying the Mediterranean.

A partial view of the Exotic Garden.

Three pictures of the Exotic Garden and its lush vegetation, including an enormous, 130-year ol Mexican cactus, the only one of its kind in Europe.

THE EXOTIC GARDEN

The Exotic Garden was created in 1913 by Prince Albert I, who was as keen on Botany as he was on Oceanography and Paleontology.

Overhanging a huge cliff-face dominating the Principality, its avenues are protected from cold winds and sunny for most of the day.

These favourable climatic conditions have enabled the acclimatization in this protected area of about 8,500 species of plants originally from the high plauteaus of Mexico, the dry areas of Arizona and the tropical and equatorial areas of Africa and South America. Over the years, succulent plants have been planted here, forming one of the richest collections in the world.

Nowadays, the Exotic Garden is one of the Principality's number one attractions, but it is also and above all a research institution where scientists and scholars from all over the world gather to attend courses.

A reserve, featuring the rarest species, enables seeds to be provided to international bodies of botanical services in countries where the flora was adapted to Monaco and which attempt to guarantee the survival of certain varieties threatened by extinction, or even extinct in the wake of natural catastrophes.

Under Prince Rainier III, the Museum of Prehistoric Anthropology has been transferred to the Exotic Garden; it was founded in 1902 by Prince Albert I and displays fossiles discovered in the caverns of the Red Rocks near the French-Italian border, not to

On these pages, other views of the Exotic Garden.

mention bones and objects from the caves of Saint-Martin, the Observatory, Bas-Moulins and Spélugues.

In the Exotic Garden, at 104 metres above sea level, the cave of the aforementioned Observatory opens up.

Partially open to the public since 1950, this habitat of our remote ancestors enjoys a constant temperature right throughout the year. Steps, bridges and ramps have been laid to facilitate visits to the rooms where countless concretions, stalactities, and stalagmites or columns have formed a magical landscape over the millenniums.

The entrance to the Wax Museum, and the façade of the Cathedral of Monaco in Neo-Romanesque style.

The Cathedral seen from the sea and a partial view of the St. Martin Gardens.

THE ROCK – WAX MUSEUM CATHEDRAL – GARDENS OF SAINT-MARTIN

The streets of the Rock pass by the old houses with their doors decorated in marble bas-reliefs and lead into picturesque squares with wells or fountains, sometimes passing under old arches.

In rue Basse, the **Wax Museum** (History Museum of the Princes of Monaco) situated under the vaults of old cellars, evokes the major events of the history of the Grimaldis.

Near the museum, a narrow covered passageway leads to a street modestly called rue de l'Eglise or Church Street. It is not just a simple chapel, but the **Cathedral of Monaco**, built between 1871 and 1877, when the Holy See decided to turn Nullius Abbey, built in 1868, into a diocese. With a seal of the 30th June 1981, Pope John Paul II raised the bishopric to archbishopric.

Dedicated to the Immaculate Conception, the Cathedral was built in white Turbie stones, according to plans by the architect Charles Lenormand in Roman-Byzantine style. It contains art treasures, including the *Retablo of Saint Nicholas* and the *Retablo of the Curate Teste*, by the artist from Nice, Louis Bréa (1443-1520).

The ambulatory of the Cathedral choir is the burial ground of defunct princes.

The main façade of the Cathedral dominating the loop and new Fontvieille district overlooks the **Saint Martin Gardens**, a magnificent explanade at the top of the Rock.

Its avenues meander through lush vegetation and flower-beds as far as the Oceanographic Museum and New Gate. They lead to the terraces and viewpoints looking out to sea and defined by Paul Valéry as "continually renewed and formed by fires".

It was in these gardens that the naturalist Jean-Baptiste Lamarck, garrisoned in Monaco at the time, became interested in the water reserves of succulent plants and developed his theory on transformism.

A marvellous view from above of the Fontvieille district and two pictures of the recently-constructed Louis II Stadium.

On the following pages: the Olympic-size swimming-pool and gymnasium of the Louis II Stadium and two views of the Fontvieille district.

FONTVIEILLE

Reclaimed with impressive works from the sea, which at this point on the coast reached depths of forty metres, the new Fontvieille district, built up against the first embankment that Prince Albert I had constructed at the beginning of the 20th Century, is without a doubt the most spectacular achievement of H.R.H. Prince Rainier III's reign.

This new embankment, protected by a dyke built before the banking up operations and supported on prefabricated caissons, covers a surface of 220,000 square metres and features, to the west of the Rock, a 55,000 metre port for pleasure boats.

Urbanization of the district is proceeding very quickly and has already enabled the laying out of a panoramic park, with a rose garden dedicated to Princess Grace, the installation of a heliport and the construction of a church and presbyterium, a school, various public services, industrial and commercial premises, council housing and luxury homes; lastly, a big tent has been set up for the International Circus Festival.

In January 1985, the **new Louis II Stadium** was inaugurated. Apart from the actual stadium itself, this sports complex seats 20,000 and includes a sports-hall, Olympic size swimming-pool, diving pool, beginners' pool, new training rooms, a school-gymnasium, 9200 square metres of office premises, 1600 square of commercial offices and four floors of parking for 1700 vehicles.

ECHAUFFEMENT CONSEILLE
10 min. d'effort
① 5' velo
② 3' corde à sauter
③ 2' barre de bois
④ 2' étirement au sol
GES

PRINCESS GRACE'S ROSE GARDEN

In the Fontvieille park, which abounds with countless species of green plants and shurbs from all four corners of the earth, Princess Grace's Rose Garden, inaugurated in 1984, was dedicated to a great lover of flowers who expressed herself so well in her book entitled "My Flower Book"; her activity continues with the International Cut Flowers Competition, which resulted from the unforgettable "Monte Carlo Flora" set up for the Monte Carlo centenary and organized every year by the Garden Club founded by her in 1968.

The garden boasts 3500 rose-bushes of over 150 varieties produced by the best European and American floriculturists.

Two pictures of the Princess Grace's Rose-Garden.

The Casino of Monte Carlo at the end of the 19th Century in a painting by Auguste Siegen.

MONTE CARLO

After the French-Monacan treaty was drawn up on the 2nd February 1861, ratifying the annexation of the Menton and Roquebrune Communes to the French Empire, the Principality was deprived of 93.75% of its territory and 83.57% of its population as well as a great deal of its agricultural and commercial resources.

In order to face this situation that had completely thrown the country's economy off-balance, Prince Charles III inaugurated a policy based entirely on tourism.

Taking the German thermal towns as an example and exploiting the northern Europeans' attraction to the "Côte d'Azur", he created a tourist resort in front of the Rock on the other side of the loop of the port; here tourists, who wish to enjoy the benefits of thalassotherapy, can also enjoy themselves, gambolling or attending top level arts festivals.

On 1st June 1866, Prince Charles III signed a decree according to which "the grounds of the Commune of Monaco, bounded by the Saint Dévote torrent, Franciosi pathway, Monaco highway and the coast shall in future be known as the Monte Carlo Quarters".

After faltering on the part of the first concessionaires, the Société des bains de mer and du cercle des étrangers began to prosper under the expert guidance of François Blanc, who rapidly made Monte Carlo the capital of elegance, art and sport.

The Hotel de Paris and other sumptuous hotels were built around the Casino, and the "Café Divan", which was later to become "Café de Paris", opened its doors. Great gardeners were called to Monaco to design the Boulingrins and create, on the arid Spélugues plateau, an oasis of exotic plants capable of giving visitors the impression of an eternal spring. Since then, the European élite has always met in Monte Carlo, where Auguste Escoffier ran the kitchens of the Grand Hotel. The architect who designed the Opera House in Paris, Charles Garnier, built an Opera House in Monte Carlo and new games rooms.

This policy of prestige was continued under Prince Albert I, especially in the field of art.

Amid the surroundings of the Garnier Music Hall, great productions followed one another and the reporter of the Figaro did not hesitate to write "Nowadays one goes to Monte Carlo as one goes to Bayreuth". The gala evenings of their new operas were attended by Georges Bizet, Charles Gounod, Jules Massenet and Camille Saint Saëns, sometimes as directors.

Soon the Diaghilev Russian ballet appeared on the scene, never to leave Monaco. They were accompanied by Nijinsky and Karsavina, and their prestigious "scenographers": Georges Roualt, Maurice

The Casino terrace in an engraving of 1866 ca.

The building of the Thermal Baths in Monte Carlo in an 1864 engraving.

Drawing of a poster on Monte Carlo nights in a water-colour of 1930 ca. by Jean Gabriel Domergue.

Walk along the Casino terrace, painted by Lelong at the beginning of the 20th Century.

Utrillo, Giorgio De Chirico, Pablo Picasso, Georges Braque, André Derain, etc.

In the Fine Arts Building, successful commedies alternated with music-hall shows, Grand Guignol presentations and the first film shows.

International speedboat and hydroplane races were held; Henri Rougier flew over the Dog's Head with his biplane while the Brazilian Santos Dumont unsuccessfully attempted to fly from Monaco to Corsica in an airship.

New sports were all the rage: tennis and golf. Twenty-three competitors from Paris, Boulogne sur mer, Brussels, Geneva, Berlin and Vienna participated in the first international grand tourism car race, the famous Monte Carlo Rally.

Between the two world wars, Monte Carlo was still at the peak of its success. Great balls organised by Jean Gabriel Domergue, the creation of the Monte Carlo Beach seaside resorts and the rapid development of a summer season with the gala evenings at the Sporting Club ensured artistic and social success. In 1929 the Monaco Grand Prix was founded; it was soon to become one of the Formula 1 World Championship races.

The pomp and ceremony continued under Prince Rainier III, who set up the districts of Portier and del Larvotto, with its long beach of fine sand; in the old station area of Monte Carlo, he authorized the construction of the Loews Hotel complex, with its outbuildings, games rooms and conference rooms.

Everybody will remember the parties and ceremonies on the occasion of Monte Carlo's Centenary, organised by a Committee chaired by Prince Grace: balls, gala evenings, exhibitions, amusements and national weeks. Nowadays tradition continues with the grand concert of the new "Ballet Company".

View from above of Monte Carlo and its port.

THE PORT

The importance of the port of Monaco was documented by ancient Greek and Roman historians and geographers, such as Hecates of Miletus, Strabo, Lucan and Ammianus Marcellinus.

In the Aeneid, Virgil recalls that Julius Caesar moored here on his way back from Gaul to Italy.

During the Middle Ages and Renaissance, galley-ships found shelter here. In fact, this port was of strategic importance until the Napoleonic Wars.

Prince Albert I modernized the port into what it is now. He had it dredged and deepened to enable heavy ships to pass. The southern quay has been specially equipped for commercial traffic; it is connected to the railway station by means of a tunnel. The northern quay is reserved for pleasure boats. Two jetties, fitted out with beacons, protect vessels against strong east winds. At the bottom of the natural loop, an esplanade has been built on piles.

At the beginning of his reign, Prince Rainier III had ports facilities, which were heavily damaged during the Second World War, repaired. With the revival and development of pleasure boats, landing stages have been built for small and medium-size boats.

The Rainier III Nautical Stadium is situated at the foot of the Albert I Quay. It is connected by a carriage road that forms part of the Grand Prix car track.

The elegant "fin de siècle" architecture of the Monte Carlo Casino by Charles Garnier.

THE CASINO

The first gambling tables were initially in a house in La Condamine in 1856, then in a hotel on Palace Square in 1858; they were then transferred to the Casino, inaugurated in 1863 on Spélugues plateau.

Two months later, François Blanc bought the concession back from François Le Febvre, founder of the "Société anonyme des bains de Monaco"; he immediately had the freshly-completed buildings extended and decorated.

For fifteen years, the Casino enjoyed a hitherto-unknown prosperity.

After the death of François Blanc, his widow Marie Blanc decided to replace it with a new building, whose design she assigned to Charles Garnier, architect of the Paris Opera House.

In May 1878, demolishing commenced. Ten months later, the new Casino and sumptuous Opera House were inaugurated.

Still today this Belle Epoque construction – world famous through postcards showing its green copper cupolas and Rococo turrets – retains the charm of those happy years.

New halls were added at a later stage: the first by Charles Garnier and the others, in 1989, by the architect Touzet who changed the façade of the Casino by building two new turrets matching those of Garnier.

Hector and Andromache, sculptured by Giorgio de Chirico in 1940, to be found in the Casino's entrance-hall.

A view of Monaco at sunset by the landscape artist Jundt; it is also hung in the entrance-hall of the Casino.

The entrance hall - In the Casino entrance-hall, crowned by a multicoloured window, twenty-eight ionic columns – forming a rectangle – are supported by a gallery lit up by sumptuous bronze candelabras.

Two large panels by the landscape artist Jundt decorate the sides. They portray, on the one hand, "*Monaco at twilight*" seen from Roquebrune beach, where fishermen light a fire and, on the other, "*The*

Two pictures of the rich decoration in the François-Médecin Room inside the Casino.

olive-trees of Cap Martin" with the town of Menton in the background.

In this entrance-hall, two exhibitions are regularly held on the Monte Carlo Ballet; the great creations of the Salle Garnier Opera; scenes of Monte Carlo Theatre, the history of Monte Carlo, etc.

The entrance hall leads into the Opera House and gambling halls.

Three views of the François-Médecin Room, with its gambling tables.

The Gambling Halls - Still retaining their overall structure and style conferred on them by Charles Garnier, the gambling halls underwent incessant changes to meet requirements.

In 1895, the Société des bains de mer was chaired by Camille Blanc, daughter of François Blanc from his first marriage.

Camille Blanc had been called upon by Prince Albert I to relaunch the Casino, after the long interim period assigned to Count Bertora in 1881, when Marie Blanc suddenly died at only forty-seven.

On her arrival, Camille Blanc entrusted the architect Schmit with changing the décor of the last gambling hall built by Charles Garnier.

In 1903, Schmit once again redecorated the white hall. The same year the smoking-room of the Casino was fitted out and decorated with magnificent stucco sculptures, pictorial compositions and gilt patterns.

Reviving a project very dear to her father but which he did not have time to accomplish, Camille Blanc decided to create a Club inside the Casino itself. Therefore new rooms were built: the famous private rooms that the Monacan François Médecin decorated in Empire style with mahogany panels featuring bronze motifs.

The panels painted by Armand Ségaud in elegant gilt frames allegorically portray the four parts of the day: "*Morning*", "*Midday*", "*Evening*" and *night*".

The roulette, trente et quarante, chemin de fer and baccara tables have witnessed the most representative 20th Century celebrities: heads of state, politicians including the imperturbable Winston Churchill, film and theatrical stars, financiers, industrialists, builders, writers and composers.

IMPAIR
MANQUE

THE GARNIER HALL

Built in six months along the lines of the Paris Opera House – albeit smaller – the Garnier Hall was decorated by the most fashionable artists of the Second Empire.

Four large statues by Jules Thomas, portraying Fame, separate four panels on the ceiling vaults whose theme is the exaltation of artistic creations: "*Comedy*" by Lix, "*Music*" by Boulanger, "*Dancing*" by Clairin and "*Singing* and *Eloquence*" by Feyen Perrin.

A huge bronze chandelier lights up the ceiling goldwork and bas-reliefs of the Hall adorned with silk tapestries and scrolls bearing the names of the greatest musicians.

At the bottom of the Hall, the Prince's box, in the form of a canopy surrounded by boxes reserved for special guests, directly faces the stage.

The Royal Family enters the Monte Carlo Opera House through a monumental door opened in the façade of the Casino, overlooking the square with the garden, where a bust by Jules Massenet was erected in 1912.

The entrance to the Garnier Room, the portrayal of the Dance and the bust of Jules Massenet.

The interior of the Garnier Room and Prince's box, crowned by the painting Feyen-Perrin portraying Singing and Eloquence and with the sculpture by Jules Thomas.

The Garnier Hall was inaugurated on the 25th January 1879 with a show preceded by a prologue from Jean Aicard, declamed by Sarah Bernhardt. It soon became one of the leading European lyric theatres where great productions were held right throughout the reign of Prince Albert and under the direction of Raoul Gunsbourg: the scenic version of the "Damnation of Faust" by Hector Berlioz, the "Minstrel of Notre Dame" by Jules Massenet, and "Penelope" by Gabriel Fauré.

The most famous singers appeared: Félia Litvine, Francesco Tamagno, Fiodor Chaliapin, Enrico Caruso, Tito Schipa etc., and so did renowned music composers such as Pietro Mascagni, Giacomo Puccini, Ruggero Leoncavallo, Luis Ganne and Igor Stravinsky.

As from 1911, Raoul Gunsbourg presented the Russian ballet which later settled in Monaco.

But the Garnier Hall was not only a privileged place for lyric art. It is equally famous for its great concerts and plays.

"Music" painted by Boulanger in 1878; a sculpture by Jules Thomas portraying "Fame", "Dancing" by Clairin and "The Comedy" painted in 1878 by Lix.

During the reigns of Prince Louis II and Prince Rainier, the tradition of new productions has been pursued.

In 1966, on the occasion of the celebration of the Centenary of Monte Carlo, spectacular evening performances were organized.

Nowadays, the Garnier Hall, with the new Monte Carlo Ballet Company, has rediscovered a form of art that ensured its success at the beginning of the century.

MOZART
VERDI
HEROLD
ROSSINI
GOUNOD
GLINKA

The Hotel de Paris: the façade facing the Place du Casino.

THE GRAND HOTELS

Monte Carlo would not have achieved such sensational success if it had not been for those structures that hotel pioneers rapidly brought to the peak of the European hotel industry at the beginning of the second half of the 19th Century.

The Grand Hotel du Boulevard des Capucines in Paris and luxury hotels in Wiesbaden and Hombourg served as models and yard sticks for the new hotel industry.

That is how **Hotel de Paris** came into being; it was inaugurated on 1st January 1864, a matter of months after the opening of the Casino, on the Spélugues plateau.

Not even a year had passed when all trade associations were back at the site to enlarge the hotel, which had proved to be too small.

The same happened regularly when extending, raising, fitting out and equipping.

For decades, architects followed one another to build the Rotunda; decorate the Empire Hall, entrance-hall, Louis XV room and verandah; raise the Rotunda, and arrange the grill terrace and its outbuilding, the Churchill Hall: Godnieau de la Bretonnièr, Dutrou, Dumoulin, Schmit, Niermans, Bruyère and Chiappori.

Every conversion and adaptation had to meet the requirements of an élite clientele. However, they were always in keeping with the taste and elegance that are a must in Monte Carlo.

In front of the Hotel de Paris, whose bar could no

The restaurant of the famous Hotel de Paris in the Louis XV room, restored by Alain Ducasse.

On the following pages, three pictures of Hotel Hermitage: the façade by the architect Marquet and two partial views of the Winter Garden.

longer accomodate its clients, the Café Divan opened in 1868. Once trasferred to its present site, it became the Grand Café of Monte Carlo, before being called **Café de Paris**. It underwent numerous alterations before being completely restored for its reopening in 1988. Done out in the style of the era in which it was created, it includes a vast entrance-hall, drugstore, gambling hall, 20th Century brasserie with open-air tables, and a room for receptions and private meals. Together with the Hotel de Paris, other grand hotels now form part of the hotel chain belonging to the Société des bains de mer: the **Monte Carlo Beach Hotel**, **Hotel Mirabeau** and **Hotel Hermitage**, bought in 1928.

Towards the end of the 19th Century, a small hotel near the Grand Hotel – now the Post Office – called the Hermitage, well-known on account of its cuisine for countless years, was transformed into a hotel restaurant, whose success goaded the owner on to building a de luxe establishment.

This gave rise to the Hotel Hermitage, designed by the Monacan architect Jean Marquet, whose magnificent façade frescoed with arches dominates the port.

The Belle Epoque Restaurant and Winter Garden, whose recent restoration won the S.B.M., the Renaissance Trophy, created by the Gault et Millau magazine and Société Vacheron-Constantin, witnessed a type of art whose safe-guarding was highly recommended by Jean Cocteau.

THE PRINCESS GRACE THEATRE

As from 1930, where the International Conference Centre stands today, the Fine Arts Theatre featured the best Parisian theatrical companies. Sacha Guitry acted as a comedian and held witty conferences.

In the nearby room, now turned into a conference room, silent films were taking their first steps and Charlie Chaplin attended the first European screening of his film "City Lights".

The completely restored Fine Arts Theatre has rediscovered its original vocation. It was inaugurated by Princess Grace one year before she died; she had agreed to it being called after her.

Apart from Monte Carlo's theatrical season, the Princess Grace Theatre houses the conferences of the Prince Peter of Monaco Foundation.

Exterior of the Princess Grace Theatre and Sphere with Sphere by Arnaldo Pomodoro displayed in the gardens of the Casino.

The Princess Grace Boulevard, and one of its futuristic fountains.

WORKS OF ART AND FOUNTAINS

The main sites of Monte Carlo, in particular the **Casino Gardens**, form a magnificent setting for a permanent sculpture exhibition, displaying works by leading contemporary artists such as Calder, Moore, Manzù, Armand, César and Pomodoro.

At the Portier crossing, the monotony of the road junction lines is broken by a Mexican style fountain, decorated with ceramics whose shapes, colours, dancing waters and lights create a harmonious effect.

Another monumental fountain in a freer style spreads out its fantastic walls and copper pillars at the end of the lane parallel to Larvotto beach, below Princess Grace Boulevard.

Three pictures of Monte Carlo at night.

MONTE CARLO BY NIGHT

"A night in Monte Carlo" is the title of a well-known song often sung during gala evenings which end up with marvellous fireworks. If, for some, Monte Carlo by night means cabarets, discotheques, the casino and Sporting Club, for others it is a precious jewelcase to be contemplated from the terrace of the Palace-Vista, hugging the mountain side, like the turret of an aircraft-carrier on the sea.

Every evening thousands of lights go on and every terrace, balcony and window offers a different view over the Monte Carlo Amphitheatre.

During the National Holiday, long garlands of electric red and white light bulbs are hung all over the town which the Bengal fires, after the firework display, drown in a haze that takes on the colours of the national flag.

CASINO
MONTE-CARLO

Two views of the Condamine residential district.

THE CONDAMINE

As from 1860, as the new town – that was to become Monte Carlo – was rapidly expanding, the Condamine district near the port and at the foot of the Moneghetti, where residential property for renting was being built, sprung up.

Until 1950, legislation limited the height of these buildings to 18.60 metres; therefore, the majority of them rose to four storeys, apart from exceptions for buildings near two roads on different levels.

Economic development requirements progressively pressurized public bodies to make this legislation more elastic until the promulgation in 1959 and 1966 of decrees that divide the Principality territory into three sectors: the safe-guarded area (the Rock and Sainte-Dévote Valley), residential area and urban area; they dictated the volume, height and soil occupation, as well as the green belt.

The height has been limited at 50 metres in the high and border areas and 35 metres in the inbetween areas.

In three decades, these new measures have completely changed the urban landscape of the Principality, from la Condamine as far as the Saint-Romain district.

From above one can admire the Saint-Roman district and the Sporting Club.

THE SAINT-ROMAN DISTRICT

The underground railway line from the French-Monacan eastern border as far as the Sainte-Dévote valley, the construction of the Portier and del Larvotto embankment and the arranging of a long sandy beach as far as the loop created by these two embankments have helped to convert the old Saint-Roman district, named after the original Christian martyr of Monaco submitted to the same torture as his companion, St. Laurent, at the time of the persecutions.

The National Fine Arts Museum, with its collections of sculptures, dolls and automatons, Hotel Beach-Plaza and its bathing facilities, the Centenary Hall which will soon be replaced by an Exhibitions Building, the huge residential complexes of Princess Grace Boulevard, the Sporting Club and its outbuildings have given new life to Monte Carlo, which was ideally represented by Prince Rainier III and Princess Grace at the ceremonies of the Monte Carlo centenary in 1966.

Situated in the French territory of Roquebrune, the property of the Société des bains de mer enabled the installation on terraces of particularly sunny tennis-courts belonging to the **Monte Carlo Country Club**, inaugurated in 1928 with the participation of the famous Suzanne Lenglen; it is where the Open Tennis Tournament is played amongst world champions.

At the other end of the embankments, between

A detail of the Sporting Club complex.

An interior of the Conference Building and the roof of this building with a mosaic done by Vasarely in 1979.

Portier and the port, stands the great **Hotel Loews** complex, with a casino, shops and restaurants; it is built on the site of Monte Carlo's old railway station.

The **Congress Centre Auditorium of Monaco**, built on piles and connected to the conference rooms of Hotel Loews, boasts numerous conference rooms, that if need be can be turned into exhibition halls and equipped with the technical equipment required for recording, the simultaneous translation of meetings and the projection of films.

The **Rainier III** Auditorium, whose seating capacity permits the organisation of the opening or closing sessions of major congresses, is fitted out with facilities that enhance the acoustics at concerts given by the Monte Carlo Philharmonic Orchestra. It can likewise be turned into a television studio.

The terrace of the Congress Centre Auditorium is adorned with a huge composition in multicoloured ceramics by Victor Vasarely.

Two pictures of the recent urban areas of Monte Carlo.

«DEO JUVANTE»

Our tour has ended. The Belle Epoque buildings, villas and houses whose façades are decorated with ceramics, mosaics or frescoes blend in with the skyscrapers that loom up at the foot of Mont-Angel and the Dog's Head as if to enable a larger number of inhabitants to admire from their own homes the unique panorama that stretches from Cap d'Ail to Cap-Martin and Bordighera with the chain of Italian Alps in the background.

The last pictures of this promenade across the Principality take us to the port quays – whose waters rock magnificent yachts, sailing boats, motorboats and fishing boats –, to Monte Carlo and du Larvotto beaches, after the bathers have left, or along the track used for the "Course dans la Cité", the day in which the inhabitants of Monaco throng the streets to watch car races featuring world champions.

We could have chosen countless other pictures to illustrate this book but the limited space available forced the editor to be selective.

It was not without regret that we had to eliminate certain photographs that document the charm and long history of the principality.

It would be a pity to end without at least mentioning the Chapel of Mercy, seat of the archiconfraternity of penitents, the National Museum of Monacan Traditions that houses countless living souvenirs of its past and the Chapel of Peace, the burial place of Prince Peter of Monaco recalled in the various epitaphs drawn up by members of the Literary and Musical Council of the principality. Mention should also be made of the Town Hall, formerly Saint Charles's College, where Guillaume Apollinaire attended high school, the Chapel of the Albert I High School which serves as a setting each year for the Baroque Music Festival, Fort Antoine, turned in summer into an

BALMORAL

Some views of the port and bathing facilities.

open-air theatre, the Louis Notari Library with its precious collections of autographs and rare books, the instrument workshop of the Rainier Musical Academy, the church dedicated to St. Dévote, patron-saint of the Principality, St. Charles's Church, parish of Monte Carlo, the Princess Antoinette Park and olive museum, Marcelle Pagnol Square, the Chapel of the Annunciation, etc.

Furthermore, we could not fail to mention the great projects under consideration such as the underground railway station, a jetty to protect cruising boats and an exhibition centre...

But despite the beauty and suggestiveness of these pictures – both those in the book and those omitted –, they only reflect a much richer reality: that of a country whose place in history and cultural development are far superior to the area it occupies; an example of the attachment to the survival and dynasty of a nation, helped by God, as is stated in the Principality of Monaco's motto.

The Open Tennis Tournament, concerts of the Philarmonic Orchestra, Monte Carlo Ballet and, above all, the Formula 1 Grand Prix – through the town – have become world famous events that attract thousands of spectators.

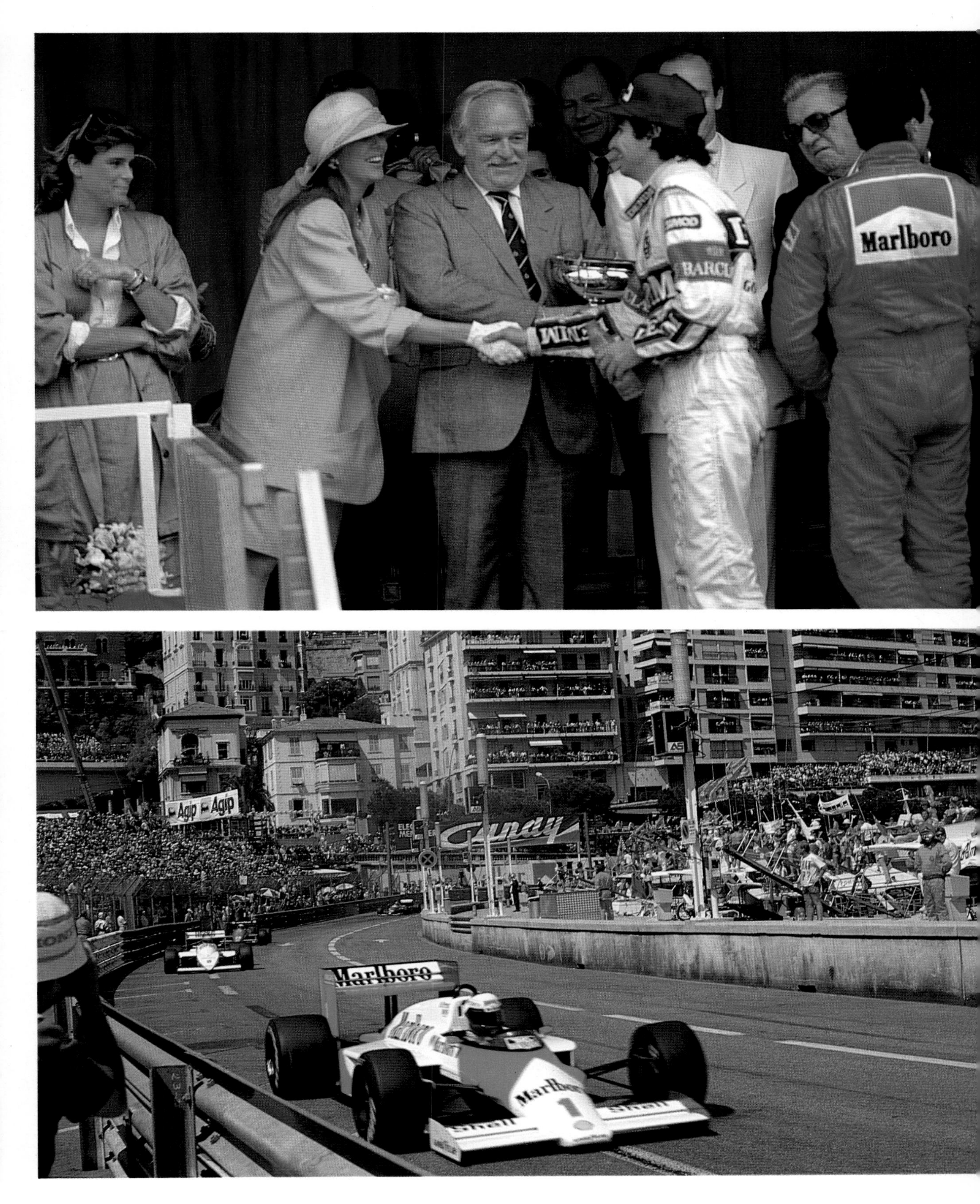
Marlboro
Agip
Agip
Marlboro
Shell

INDEX

E-mail: bonechi@bonechi.it Internet: www.bonechi.it

Printed in Italy by Centro Stampa Editoriale Bonechi

Translated by Susan Fraser, Studio Comunicare Florence.

Photographic service by Gianni Dagli Orti.

ISBN 88-7009-418-9

* * *